The Email Prospecting Playbook:

How to Quickly and Predictably Reawaken Dead Leads, Generate New Client Opportunities and Convert Not-Yet-Ready Prospects Into Freelance Writing Clients

ED GANDIA

A Note From Ed

My results and those of my coaching clients are not typical. I'm not implying that you'll duplicate them. I've had the benefit of practicing email prospecting for 17 years. The average person who buys any "how to" information gets little or no results. I'm using these references for example purposes only. Your results will vary and depend on many factors, including but not limited to your background, experience and work ethic. All business entails risk, as well as massive effort, action…and a good dose of blood, sweat and tears.

ISBN: 1544028180
ISBN-13: 978-1544028187

CONTENTS

Introduction

I'm not much of a forecaster. But I'm going to go out on a limb and predict that LinkedIn won't be around in 45 years.

Neither will Facebook, Twitter, Snapchat or Upwork.

Sure, some byproducts of these platforms might exist. Maybe with built-in artificial intelligence and an optional flux capacitor.

But they won't look anything like they do today.

Now compare that with email—a technology that's been around for 45 years (give or take a few, since the technology wasn't really "invented"; it evolved over the years, taking hold in the early 1970s).

Forty-five years in technology is like 300 years in any other industry.

Yet to this day, email is one of the most powerful prospecting tools ever invented. It has survived numerous shifts in the world of technology. It even survived social media and SMS, which many predicted would make it obsolete.

Email enables you to prospect for clients effectively and efficiently. Especially when you're an established freelance writer or copywriter (you'll soon see why).

In fact, according to research from personalization software company Monetate, email marketing drives more conversions than any other marketing channel, including search and social.

And when email prospecting is done right, the return on investment (mainly of your time and effort) can be astronomical. The Direct Marketing

Association pegs the average ROI of email marketing at 3,800 percent.

Despite the obvious advantages of email over other marketing channels, many "experts" continue to claim that email effectiveness is rapidly declining.

How could anyone claim that in the face of so much evidence to the contrary?

Well, there is some truth to that statement. *Untargeted* email marketing is what's truly on the decline.

By "untargeted" I'm referring to mass email broadcasts that fail to take into account the individual recipient's challenges, needs and wants.

Targeted, relevant and personalized email marketing, on the other hand, is working like gangbusters. In fact, the more generic and irrelevant emails other marketers and freelancers send to their prospects, the more your targeted and personalized emails will stand out.

Because in a noisy world where most marketing messages sound the same, the freelancer who can create a truly personalized, relevant and one-to-one (as opposed to "one to many") email will get the prospect's attention.

And here's the great news for you: As a freelance professional, you have the ability to handcraft personalized and relevant emails that get noticed, get opened and get a positive response.

Because unlike big companies that pretty much *have to* automate every aspect of their marketing, you have the time and the insider knowledge to write and send powerful, one-to-one messages that just *beg to be answered.*

In this book, I'm going to show you a simple system and strategy for turning short and simple emails into your most powerful client-generating tool.

It truly is a playbook. I'm going to detail what to do and what to send... and in what order to do all this.

Follow this simple method. Be diligent and be patient. I think you'll be surprised by your results.

The System at a Glance

This email prospecting playbook has three key steps:

1. Activate dead leads and dormant clients
2. Generate new leads
3. Nurture not-yet-ready leads

For our purposes, here's how I define each of these prospect categories:

- **Dead leads:** Prospects who indicated interest in your services at some point but never turned into clients. Also, you stopped following up long ago. So they'd probably *not* remember your name if you were to contact them today.

- **Dormant clients:** These are clients you worked with in the past that are currently inactive. (It's been a while since you worked with them.)

- **New leads:** Prospects that have recently expressed an interest in your services. Could be an inbound lead or a lead you generated through outreach efforts.

- **Not-yet-ready leads:** Prospects that have expressed interest in your services but that weren't ready to hire you at the time.

NOTE: I use the terms "lead" and "prospect" interchangeably. For our purposes, they mean the same thing.

When you follow this playbook for the first time, it's important to follow this specific order.

There's a good reason for that. Reaching out to dead leads and dormant clients using the approach I'm about to teach you will potentially uncover some immediate project opportunities. These projects could bring in some much-needed income quickly, which will then buy you some time to prospect for new leads.

And as some of these new leads turn out to be not-yet-ready leads (interested but not yet ready to hire you), you'll have a system in place for staying in touch with them until they *are* ready.

In the next chapter, we'll dive deeper into the first category: activating dead leads and dormant clients.

Chapter 1:

Activate Dead Leads and Dormant Clients

The Power of Quick Wins

Ever go on a diet?

If you're like me, you've probably tried more than one approach to losing weight and getting physically fit.

Think back to the diet and exercise programs you stuck with the longest. The ones that actually worked.

I bet they were hard at first.

So why did you keep going? Why did you persist, despite the fact that you were hungry all the time or didn't feel like going to the gym?

You probably pushed through these initial obstacles because you saw some results quickly.

Maybe you lost 10 lbs. in the first couple of weeks. Or the jeans that used to be tight the previous month now fit perfectly. Or a good friend commented on how great you looked.

That's the power of quick wins!

Most of us will keep working hard if we can see tangible results early in the game, when we're most susceptible to getting off track and quitting.

And that's why my email prospecting playbook starts with contacting dead leads and dormant clients. Because if you're an established freelance writer, this is where you're most likely to find your quick wins.

They may not be dream projects. They may not pay you record fees. But they could generate cash quickly, boost your self-confidence and buy you some time to find even better opportunities.

Plus, these are the easiest emails to write. They're incredibly short and simple. And once you start seeing results, you're going to want to send out more of them.

So let's start there. Let's start with a nine-word email.

The Nine-Word Email

The nine-word email is one of the most effective email prospecting strategies you'll ever use. You'll be hard pressed to find another email structure that will generate a higher response rate.

Made famous by marketing legend Dean Jackson, the nine-word email is designed to mimic the kind of conversation you would have with someone you know if you ran into them at, say, the grocery store.

It touches on something that's relevant to the prospect or client. The message makes it patently clear that this email was written specifically for them (that it's a one-to-one email). And it asks a question at the end that begs for an answer.

Before we get into actual examples, it's important to understand the psychology behind the nine-word email.

Imagine you strike up a conversation with someone at a friend's party—someone you just met that evening. Her name is Jill, and during your conversation she mentions that she and her husband are thinking about visiting California wine country.

You immediately get excited because you've been to wine country half a dozen times. So you give Jill a list of recommended wineries, quaint inns and excellent restaurants to consider.

Jill is ecstatic to talk with someone who knows this much about the area. She thanks you numerous times for the tips and recommendations.

A few weeks later, you run into Jill at the grocery store. And after greeting her, you ask her a simple question:

Are you still thinking about going to wine country this summer?

Doesn't that sound like a natural question to ask? You're bringing up something relevant from your conversation at the party. So it feels like a sincere way to start a new conversation.

Do You Still Want Those Sweaters?

OK, let's take another example. This one's a bit "out there," so bear with me.

Say you work at the men's department in Nordstrom. A customer comes in (let's call him Mr. Smith) looking for a brown sweater. You help him select a few options. He tries some on in the dressing room and sets two sweaters by the register.

"I'm not sure which one I want," he tells you. "Let me look around a bit more and come back."

"Of course, you reply. "Take your time, Mr. Smith."

You turn to help another customer. And an hour later you realize that Mr. Smith never came back. The sweaters he tried on are still sitting by the register.

Later that afternoon during your lunch break, you run into Mr. Smith at the food court.

"Hey, Mr. Smith! Great to run into you here," you say.

If you were to ask him a question, what would that be?

How about: "Do you still want those sweaters?"

Or maybe: "Are you still thinking about buying one of those sweaters?"

Again, I know this is a silly hypothetical example. But can you see how such a scenario might play out in real life?

Essentially, here's what happened in both of these hypothetical situations:

1. You had a conversation with someone.
2. You discussed X.
3. You ran into them later.
4. You asked them about X.

The Standard Approach Is Not Working!

What does this have to do with prospecting for freelance clients?

Think about how you might typically prospect online. Maybe you send out a monthly newsletter that includes a plug about your services.

Or maybe you send "emails of introduction" explaining what you do and whom you serve.

Or maybe you post a blurb about what you do on one of your social networks, hoping to attract some prospects who might need these services.

In all these cases, you're sending a broadcast. A "one to many" email (one message to many people).

We all know how these methods work. It's like throwing spaghetti at the wall. Throw enough spaghetti and a few noodles might stick.

Maybe.

But what if you took a different approach? What if instead of taking a one-to-many approach you instead tried to start a conversation with one prospect at a time?

That's where the nine-word email comes in.

The Nine-Word Email Template

The nine-word email is one of the most elegant conversation starters you could ever use.

Let me first give you an example. We'll then break down the components and discuss the different flavors you can deploy (and when each flavor is most appropriate).

> *SUBJECT: White papers*
>
> *Hi Joan,*
>
> *Are you still thinking about hiring an outside white paper writer this year?*
>
> *Ed*

Why does this email work so well?

First, let's point out the obvious. This particular script is longer than nine words. And that's OK. Because the nine-word email is more of a concept than a literal formula. The idea behind "nine words" is to keep your email extremely short.

So short, in fact, that you're going to feel uncomfortable sending it at first.

But it's not just about brevity. What makes a nine-word email incredibly effective is that when done right, it follows Dean Jackson's "SPEAR" formula:

- **S**hort,
- **P**ersonal,
- **E**xpecting
- **A** reply

The personalization in the example above is obvious when you understand the context. In this example Joan had expressed interest in hiring a writer for some white paper work.

She and I had some email dialogue about it three months ago. We also got on the phone to discuss her project.

But then she disappeared. (Ever have that happen to you?!)

I followed up a few times but never heard back. (Darn it!!)

Now that a few months have passed, I'm touching base again. But rather than going into a long and drawn-out follow-up email, I'm getting right to the point. I'm pointing to the "thing" about which she had expressed interest.

The sweaters still sitting by the cash register.

In fact, in my mind I'm pretending that I just ran into her at the food court. I'm imagining what that conversation might look like in real life. Maybe something like:

> Me: "Hey! Joan, right?"

> Joan: "Yes, hi! What a surprise to run into you here, Ed. How are you?"

> Me: "Great! Business is good. Just wrapped up a great year. How about you?"

> Joan: "Oh, crazy as always. Never enough hours in the day! You know how it is."

> Me: "I hear ya! Hey, that reminds me: Are you still thinking about hiring an outside white paper writer this year?"

Doesn't that sound like a very normal and natural conversation? Yes, I realize that you're probably not going to run into a prospect at the food court or the grocery store. Especially if you live in Los Angeles and Joan lives in New York.

But just pretend for a second that this actually happened.

Wouldn't this "flow" feel natural?

It pretty much mirrors a conversation I would have if I ran into someone I haven't talked to in a while.

Now, think about the last question I asked Joan. The "Are you still thinking about hiring an outside white paper writer this year?"

Can you imagine a scenario where Joan would abruptly walk away without answering your question?

No, that would be weird for both of us. I can pretty much guarantee that she'd answer the question if she were standing in front of me. Because the question begs to be answered.

That's the "expecting a reply" part.

OK, back to the previous email script sample:

SUBJECT: White papers

Hi Joan,

Are you still thinking about hiring an outside white paper writer this year?

Ed

Other key points to note:

- There's no fluff and no wasted words.

- I'm also not "warming up" the prospect with small talk, which is what everyone does! ("Hope you're having a great summer so far...") Subconsciously, this shows the prospect that I respect their time. (Yes, sometimes you have to add some context, but I'll show you more effective ways to do that.)

- I'm not dancing around the issue or using meaningless follow-up ("...I'd be happy to discuss your needs...") or "let me know" language ("...Let me know if there's anything I can do to help you with any writing projects...").

- I don't need this email to do all the work. I'm not trying to land work. I'm simply trying to restart the conversation. The selling happens later, but I need to rekindle the dialogue first!

- Finally, note that the subject line is very direct. That's the opposite of what we'd normally use in a marketing broadcast, where we're trying to arouse curiosity with the subject line.

Now that you've seen a sample nine-word email, let's go over the different flavors you can employ and when each works best.

Flavor #1: "Are You Still?"

The example we just reviewed (Joan, who was looking for a white paper writer at some point) is a classic example of the "Are you still?" flavor of nine-word emails.

Here are some examples:

- Are you still thinking about working with an outside writer?

- Are you still considering getting some writing help?

- Are you still interested in launching a newsletter this year?

- Are you still interested in working together on any of the following?

- Are you still interested in scheduling a call to discuss Q1 projects?

This flavor works well when you have some information from a previous exchange and you're using that as the purpose of your follow-up.

It's appropriate for all four groups we covered earlier: current clients, dormant clients, dead leads and not-yet-ready (NYR) leads. But it's much more effective in situations where you have some background or context.

So in cases of a dead lead or dormant client where you have little or nothing to go on, this flavor may not work as well, and flavor #2 (coming up next) would be more effective.

How to Add Context

Sometimes adding context to your nine-word email can help with response. For instance, in the earlier example with Joan and the white papers, you could "append" your nine-word to the original email thread under it.

By "append" I mean resuming that previous email exchange. For example, if you and Joan corresponded about this four months ago and you still have the existing email thread with your back-and-forth communications, simply reply to that last email and add your nine-word email to the top.

That way Joan can see the context of your nine-word email and can "place" you more easily.

If you don't have an email thread you can reference, it's OK to add that context. But consider adding it as a P.S. at the bottom of your email. That way your context doesn't distract the recipient from the question.

For example:

SUBJECT: Your newsletter

Hi Maria,

Are you still interested in launching a newsletter this year?

Ed Gandia

P.S. I'm the writer Brenda Stevens referred to you last October.

Flavor #2: "Are You?"

This flavor of nine-word email is useful when you're not entirely sure what (if any) needs your client or prospect has.

Unlike "Are you still?" emails (flavor #1), which point to something specific the prospect or client had identified or mentioned at some point, "Are you?" emails make an educated guess about a current or upcoming need as a way to start the conversation.

Here are some examples:

- Are you planning on publishing some white papers this year?

- Are you thinking about launching a newsletter this year?

- Are you thinking about getting outside writing help in the next few months?

- Do you still have a potential need for a content marketing writer?

For example:

SUBJECT: Marketing collateral

Hi Christine,

Are you planning on publishing new marketing collateral this year?

Ed Gandia

This flavor can work well with all four groups. But it's especially effective with dormant clients and dead leads you haven't contacted in a while (and therefore don't have much to go on).

Here again, you can append your nine-word email to a past email thread you had with your contact, even if your new message is unrelated. Otherwise, consider adding a short P.S. to remind them who you are.

Or you could use a simple email signature that includes a title, a description of what you do, or even your target market or specialty. That way the recipient can easily connect the dots.

For example:

> Ed Gandia
> Copywriter for Enterprise Software Companies
>
> June Evans
> Healthcare Writer
>
> Scott Marshall
> White Paper Writer

Flavor #3: "Would You?"

This flavor is ideal when you're not sure what the prospect or client might need. However, based on what you know about the prospect, you offer a service they might be interested in exploring.

This flavor can work with all four groups, but it's typically most effective with people you've been in touch with or who would recognize your name: current clients, dormant clients, NYR leads.

Don't be afraid to send it to a dead lead, however. If the service you point out happens to be something that's on their radar screen, it could start an immediate email conversation.

Here are a few examples:

- Would you be interested in working with me on your new marketing collateral?

- Would you like to get your newsletter launched by the end of the quarter?

- Would you like some help planning your next white paper?

- Would you like me to help you write another product backgrounder?

Notice how this flavor takes more of a consultative approach. It works well when you're proposing an idea, something you suspect would help the client. Or when you believe that a current or dormant client could benefit from the idea ... but they've been too busy with other things to think about it.

Sample script:

> SUBJECT: *Your marketing collateral*
>
> *Hi Mike,*
>
> *Would you be interested in working with me on your new marketing collateral?*
>
> *Ed*

And again, the nine-word email is a concept, not a strict word-count rule. So you could add some context or credibility like this:

> SUBJECT: *White papers*
>
> *Hi Joe,*
>
> *I've been working with a number of SaaS clients to help them write persuasive white papers.*
>
> *Would you be interested in discussing some white paper ideas?*
>
> *Ed*

Flavor #4: "Have You?"

This is yet another consultative nine-word email type. It proposes an idea that would be relevant and beneficial to the client or prospect:

- Have you considered writing some customer success stories to highlight how [your client's product or service] generates results?

- Have you thought about repurposing some of your webinars into white papers or e-books?

- Have you considered publishing a short newsletter to stay top of mind with longer-term prospects?

Here again, it typically works in situations where the recipient would recognize your name. But if you can discern a possible need based on some basic research, it could be just as effective with a dead lead.

Here's what a typical script would look like:

SUBJECT: Content repurposing idea

Hi Jamie,

Have you thought about repurposing some of your webinars into white papers or e-books?

Ed

Here's another variation of that idea:

SUBJECT: Content repurposing idea

Hi Jamie,

I've been working with a number of SaaS clients to repurpose some of their marketing content.

Have you thought about repurposing some of your webinars into white papers or e-books?

Ed

Flavor #5: "Do You?"

This final flavor represents a very strategic way to throw spaghetti at the wall. It's most effective with dead leads, dormant clients and maybe even NYR leads—groups on which you may not have enough information to use a different flavor.

It flat-out asks if they do a certain thing, have a particular challenge, have a specific need or have something coming up you might be able to help them with.

Some examples:

- Do you publish white papers?

- Do you ever work with outside writers?

- Do you produce marketing materials for your reseller partners?

- Do you need some help writing marketing materials?

In some cases, however, it can even work well with dormant clients—especially when you're addressing something you're not sure about.

Or when you're checking in to see if something they mentioned a few months ago is still a possibility.

Or even when you've started offering a new service and you want to see if some of your old clients would be interested in learning more about it.

Script example:

SUBJECT: Writing help

Hi Brandon,

Do you need some help writing marketing materials?

Ed

Here again, in cases where the recipient may not recognize you—and when you don't have an old email thread you can use—you could add a quick P.S. to jog their memory:

SUBJECT: Writing help

Hi Brandon,

Do you need some help writing marketing materials?

Ed Gandia

P.S. We met at the ABIC meeting last September.

Here's another example that landed one of my coaching clients a project within one hour of sending the email:

SUBJECT: Projects

Hi Robert,

I'm mapping out my schedule for the coming months.

Any projects I should have on my radar?

Kate

As you can probably see by now, the possibilities with these nine-word emails are endless.

Don't let their simplicity fool you. These emails are very powerful. But they require some thought before sending.

Take the time to think through each prospect and client carefully before drafting your script. Think through all the different flavors and your history with the individual. And come up with a message that sounds natural and begs for a reply.

Remember the SPEAR criteria:

- **S**hort,
- **P**ersonal,
- **E**xpecting
- **A** reply

A Word on Subject Lines

A key component of email marketing success is using the right subject line. Nine-word emails are not exempt from this requirement. You have to get this component right for your email to be effective.

Luckily, you don't have to get creative with your subject line. In a nine-word email, your subject line needs to be bland and direct, which is the opposite of what we often use in marketing broadcasts, where we're trying to arouse curiosity.

Think about it. What kind of subject line would you use if you were emailing a friend? You'd probably use a very straightforward subject line, wouldn't you?

Maybe something like:

Dinner on Sunday

Lunch

Dog shelter

Getting together

Cindy's birthday

Beach trip

Guacamole recipe

And of course, each of these subject lines would correspond perfectly to the message inside the email.

For example, you'd never use the subject line "Dog shelter" if you're emailing your friend Brian asking him for his famous guacamole recipe.

You'd also never bait and switch Brian with a "curiosity" subject line such as "What in the world??" when your email was asking him if he could support your daughter by buying some Girl Scout cookies.

In that situation you'd probably use "Cookies" as your subject line, wouldn't you?

It's the same with a nine-word email. You have to keep your subject lines direct and natural. Note some of the subject lines I used in the earlier nine-word email examples:

> White papers

> Your newsletter

> Your marketing collateral

> Writing help

Again, nine-word emails are conversation starters—very reliable ones. Very rarely will they generate immediate work on their own.

But that's OK. I'd rather have a system for sparking numerous conversations than an unreliable system for generating work quickly. Because I know that every great client relationship starts out as a simple conversation.

Put these emails to the test. I think you'll be very surprised with your results.

Chapter 2:

Generate New Leads

In the previous chapter I showed you how to revive dead leads and reconnect with dormant clients.

But when the prospect has no idea who you are, it's best to take a different approach. That's what we'll cover in this chapter.

What NOT to Do!

First, let's look at the typical prospecting emails your potential clients get every week from vendors they've never worked with. This is an actual example that landed in my inbox recently (yes, I collect these things!).

SUBJECT: Expert Outsourced 24/7 Helpdesk

Good Morning,

I would like to introduce Visiotech to you. We are one of England's leading providers of expert outsourced 24/7 IT, Wi-Fi and technology services providing remote helpdesk support using our technical operations centre.

Overflow Helpdesk Support and Out Of Hours Helpdesk Support:

We provide a completely white labelled service to enhance your existing helpdesk team. Currently we support over 60 IT, Telecoms, Wi-Fi and Software developers.

We provide a 1st and 2nd line technical support team to work with you. A great solution for increasing demand for support outside of normal business hours. We are also able to provide a 24/7 multi lingual service and Network Operations service which may offer additional benefits for your customer base.

We have moved across the pond:

We have recently opened an office in Savannah, Georgia and we are keen to discuss our services with companies in your area.

How does Outsourcing your helpdesk benefit your business?

1. It reduces your staffing costs. Why hire another member of staff, if you can outsource all of your calls for less? We are normally between 25-50% cheaper than an in-house option.

2. It expands your opening hours. We have a technical operations centre which is open 24/7/365.

3. It will improve your customer experience. Are you taking multiple calls from clients, but can't get back to them as quick as you would like? Well now you have a team of 30 well-spoken staff taking your support calls for you. Have an important meetings? No problem, your helpdesk has your back.

Outsourcing front-line services is a gamble and one I had looked into previously with little to convince me my clients would be looked after. However, after initially meeting with Jon at Visiotech and finding a synergy in our customer service ethos, I felt I could move my front line support helpdesk over to Jon's team. The feedback from my clients was positive from the outset.

Director - Red Cube IT

So if you would like to explore options of utilising our UK based 24/7 technical service desk, please do not hesitate to contact a member of our solutions team.

Kind Regards,

Lisa Chandler

What's wrong with this prospecting email?

Gee, where do I start?! Not only is it way too long, but it's completely irrelevant to my business, it's not personalized, and it's essentially a sales presentation in email form.

In other words, Lisa is trying to deliver the whole pitch in one message.

There are other problems with the message and the strategy, but those are the biggest.

Let's look at another example:

SUBJECT: Phone call on Monday at 2:00 PM

Hi Ed,

How are you? I hope this email finds you well!

I'd like to ask, would you be interested in combining LinkedIn, voice and email campaigns to drive potential clients to your business?

I believe we can help you in developing warm leads and in setting up appointments on your behalf. We can act as your professional marketing arm while you focus on closing deals.

We have experience running campaigns for businesses in your vertical. Our data capabilities allow us to create contact lists according to your target industries.

If it's something interesting, kindly let me know if you're available for a call today or the following? Just let me know a good time that works with your schedule and the best number to reach you.

Brad Jensen

This one is better than the first example. It's shorter and more inviting.

But when I received it, I could immediately tell that it's not relevant to what I do. The sender didn't take the time to understand my business before pitching his service. Otherwise he would have realized that I'm not in his target market.

Then there's the subject line. Brad took a bait-and-switch approach, making me believe that this was about an appointment I had next Monday afternoon. Yet the email had nothing to do with that. In fact, he didn't even ask for a call on Monday at 2 p.m.!

A Better Way to Contact Cold Leads

There's a much better way to generate leads with cold prospects. It's called "warm email prospecting." Mainly because it's the opposite of cold calling. And it's very different from your standard, generic email prospecting.

Unlike most marketing emails, warm emails employ three key psychological triggers:

1.   Personalization. The email was written specifically for the prospect.

2.   Relevance. The email is directly relevant to the prospect's work.

3.   Brevity. The email is short and to the point. Specifically, 125 words or less.

When these three triggers are in place, your warm email will stand out from 99 percent of all marketing emails in your prospect's inbox.

Why? ***Because it shows that you've done your homework!*** And that alone gives you a much higher chance of getting a response.

Just like with a nine-word email, the goal of warm email is simply to start a conversation, not to land a project.

Essentially, you want the prospect to respond with a question or statement that indicates some level of interest.

But unlike a nine-word email, a warm email is a little longer. That's because the prospect doesn't know you. So you need to offer a little more to show why he or she should respond.

The Warm Email Template

Over the years, I've identified four key structural components to a warm email and put them into a template, as follows:

SUBJECT LINE: [Meaningful Connection]

EMAIL BODY:

[Meaningful Connection]

[Value Statement]

[Credibility URL]

[Soft Invitation to Connect]

Let's quickly review each of these components:

+ **Meaningful Connection:** A statement that ties what you do to something you noticed about that particular prospect. It does *not* need to be a person or event. It can be something you noticed on the prospect's website. Or a company attribute that would make the prospect need someone with your skill set. (More about this in a minute.)

+ **Value Statement:** A sentence or two that explains what you do, for whom you do it and why you're different from many competitors. It can also explain why that difference matters.

+ **Credibility URL:** A link to your "About Me" page, some relevant samples, testimonials, a success story about how you helped a client solve a challenge, or anything that would help you sound credible. It doesn't have to be a link, however. It can be a list of recent clients. Or a description of an award you've received. Or a big accomplishment, number of years of experience or information about your unique background.

+ **Soft Invitation to Connect:** No need to be wordy or elaborate. Keep it low-key. And consider using a question. You could ask, "Should we connect?" or maybe, "Would it make sense to schedule a brief call soon?"

Again, it's important to keep your email short and to the point: **125 words or less!** Remember: *Brevity* is one of the key psychological triggers!

Meaningful Connections

Most of these components are relatively straightforward, except perhaps for "meaningful connections."

What kind of meaningful connection are we talking about, exactly? There are four basic types you can use in your email. But in this book I want to focus on the two most common types, because they're also the easiest to use:

1. Point to a "trigger attribute"
2. Name a relevant client or accomplishment, or relevant knowledge or experience

Let's look at each of these individually.

Point to a Trigger Attribute

Trigger attributes are attributes about a prospect that could trigger a need for your services. They're based on something the prospect has been doing for a while (a trend) *or* something that is just part of who the prospect is or what he or she (or the organization) stands for.

Here are some examples:

- "Hey, Mr. Prospect: I noticed that you have quite a few _____ posted on your website."

- "Hey, Ms. Prospect: I noticed that you're starting to really go after the _____ market."

- "Hey, Mr. Prospect: I noticed that you do a lot of work in this area..."

For example:

SUBJECT LINE: Been watching your Big Data webinar series

Hi Max,

I've been watching your recent Big Data webinar series. I couldn't agree more about the importance of moving this discussion to the boardroom.

I'm writing because I'm a technology veteran who works with enterprise software companies to repurpose business white papers into webinar content, video scripts, road shows and other compelling content formats. I've worked with ABC Data, XYZ Tech and others on similar projects.

Here are some samples of my work: [URL].

I'd love to chat briefly and run some ideas by you. If this sounds interesting, let me know when would be a good day and time to discuss.

Here's another example:

SUBJECT: *I keep seeing info about Xtronix monitors*

Hi Tina,

I keep seeing your name everywhere (I do a lot of writing work in the waterworks and wastewater treatment industry). I'm very impressed with what I've read about your new line of Xtronix wastewater treatment monitors. Definitely a game changer!

I was curious: Do you ever work with outside writers for any of your marketing materials? And if you do, I'd love to know what it would take to be considered for a future project.

I specialize in helping companies in the water treatment industry write marketing content and sales copy. You can learn more about my experience here:

[URL]

Would it make sense to connect?

Name a Relevant Client or Accomplishment, or Relevant Knowledge or Experience

This kind of meaningful connection can be very powerful, yet it's one of the most *underused* approaches in warm email prospecting.

It's all about pointing out something *relevant* about your background, experience or skill set that would be attractive to the prospect, and then briefly explaining how it could be relevant and valuable to him or her.

Note: It does *not* need to be about your freelance experience. It can be about something outside your freelance career.

Examples:

- I was a high school teacher for 22 years.
- I was an analyst for Forrester Research for seven years.
- I was in hotel management for 12 years.
- I've worked in and around the renewable energy industry for eight years.
- As a journalist, I've been writing about renewable energy for the past four years.
- I'm a Salesforce.com certified developer, so I understand _____.
- I've written for XYZ Co. and ABC, Inc.
- My family has been in the auto parts industry for over 60 years.
- I'm a passionate gardener and homesteader.
- We homeschooled our three children through middle school.

Here's an example:

SUBJECT: Love what you're doing with Sparx

Hi Belinda,

I've been following the growth of your Sparx online learning initiative. I'm very impressed with what you're doing here and the impact it's having on high school students.

I'm not sure how you're handling the writing of your marketing content, but I'd love to know what it would take to be considered for some of these needs.

I was a high school teacher for 22 years and now focus on writing marketing content for training and online learning companies. I use my experience as an educator and avid proponent of online learning to deliver persuasive writing that hits the mark.

You can learn more about me and my work here: [URL].

Should we connect?

Your Objective Is to Start a Conversation

Again, your goal with a warm email is not to land a client. There's no way an email can do that kind of heavy lifting.

Instead your goal is the same as that of a nine-word email—to start a conversation. Ideally, you want the prospect to respond with a question or statement that indicates some level of interest.

For example:

"Interesting. Tell me more about what you do."

"We may have a need for someone with your skills. Can you send me more information about your fees?"

"We were working with another writer, but she recently left to work full time with another client. Can you touch base with me in three weeks? I'll be in a better place to discuss at that time."

Once you get that kind of response, you can work to take the conversation to a phone call. And that's where the meaningful dialogue will take place that can lead to a project.

Don't Overcomplicate Things!

One of the best things about this prospecting approach is its simplicity.

You don't need to do a lot of research on your prospect to make that relevant connection in your email. In fact, that's one of the most common misconceptions about what it takes to craft a solid warm email. Consider this example:

SUBJECT LINE: Your recent white papers

Hi Jennifer,

I've come across your website a few times over the years because I've done work in the corporate health and wellness area. As I looked through your site this morning, I noticed that you're starting to publish a lot of white papers.

Do you have an internal resource for this? Or are you working with an outside professional?

I ask because I'm a business writer who specializes in white papers, e-books and long-format reports. Because of my experience in the wellness field, I may be able to help you get these pieces produced faster and more cost-effectively.

Here's a link to some samples of my work: [URL].

Should we connect?

Notice in this example that just pointing to something you saw on their site that's relevant to the work you do can be enough, as long as you can tie it together in a natural and authentic way.

Also, your email doesn't need to be very long. And better yet, you can reuse most of your email copy from one prospect to the next!

For instance, when you look at some of these examples, note that you could easily reuse about 80 percent of the copy if you're focused on a particular industry or target market:

SUBJECT LINE: Been watching your Big Data webinar series

Hi Max,

I've been watching your recent Big Data webinar series. I couldn't agree more about the importance of moving this discussion to the boardroom.

Reusable

> *I'm writing because I'm a technology veteran who works with enterprise software companies to repurpose business white papers into webinar content, video scripts, road shows and other compelling content formats. I've worked with ABC Data, XYZ Tech and others on similar projects.*
>
> *Here are some samples of my work: [URL].*
>
> *I'd love to chat briefly and run some ideas by you. If this sounds interesting, let me know when would be a good day and time to discuss.*

Another example:

I keep seeing your name everywhere (I do a lot of writing work in the waterworks and wastewater treatment industry). I'm very impressed with what I've read about your new line of Xtronix wastewater treatment monitors. Definitely a game changer!

Reusable

> *I was curious: Do you ever work with outside writers for any of your marketing materials? And if you do, I'd love to know what it would take to be considered for a future project.*
>
> *I specialize in helping companies in the water treatment industry write marketing content and sales copy. You can learn more about me here:*
>
> *[URL]*
>
> *Would it make sense to connect?*

And yet another example:

SUBJECT: Love what you're doing with Sparx

Hi Belinda,

I've been following the growth of your Sparx online learning initiative. I'm very impressed with what you're doing here and the impact it's having on high school students.

Reusable

> *I'm not sure how you're handling the writing of your marketing content, but I'd love to know what it would take to be considered for some of these needs.*
>
> *I was a high school teacher for 22 years and now focus on writing marketing content for training and online learning companies. I use my experience as an educator and avid proponent of online learning to deliver persuasive writing that hits the mark.*
>
> *You can learn more about me and my work here: [URL].*
>
> *Should we connect?*

This is yet another reason why it pays to keep your business focused. When you focus on just one or two target markets, project types, or some other type of targeting, your prospecting becomes a lot easier—and much more effective!

Chapter 3:

Nurture Not-Yet-Ready Leads

Ever go weeks prospecting for clients without something to show for it?

You "knock" on what seems like a ton of doors. But no one seems to be interested.

And when you finally get a response, it's something along the lines of "I'll keep your information on file..."

It's exhausting, isn't it?

Well, there's a reason why this happens. According to research by business development agency Vorsight, only 3 percent of qualified prospects are *actively* searching for someone who provides your services.

So yes, at any given time, only about 3 percent of qualified prospects in your target market are actively looking for a freelance writer or copywriter.

That means that just three out of 100 actually have a need AND are looking for a freelancer who does what you do.

These "hot" prospects are a needle in the haystack!

What about the other 97?

According to that same research, 40 of them will *probably* have a need for your services sometime in the next few months. These are your not-yet-ready (NYR) prospects.

And the rest—a whopping 57 of them—won't be looking anytime soon!

Those aren't great odds, are they?

You're working hard to find a few gems (the 3 percent). And even when you find them... there's no guarantee that they'll hire you.

Now, look. When you're starting out, there's no way around this.

You have to pay the price. You have to knock on 43,286 doors. Because you're looking for those hot prospects who have work TODAY.

But once you've landed a few clients and are somewhat established... is there a better way of doing this? Or are you doomed to prospect like a crazy person forever?

Fortunately, there *is* a better way.

And it's all about staying in touch with that "40 percent" group—the one most freelancers ignore.

Where the Real Gold Is

Spending tons of time and energy looking for the magical 3 percent is a lot of work. But what if you instead looked for the group that's right behind them—the NYR prospects who will probably be ready soon or at some point in the near future?

And what if you stayed in touch with that group until they were ready for you?

When you go about your prospecting this way, you'll automatically find the 3 percent who are ready today. And you'll be the first person these prospects turn to when the timing is right.

Over the years I've found that much of the difference between just "getting by" and earning an executive-level income as a freelance professional lies in what you do with prospects who are not ready to hire you today.

I call it "lead nurturing." And once I saw the impact this kind of follow-up had on my income, it quickly became a critical part of my marketing and sales process as a freelancer.

Whom Should You Nurture?

Which prospects should you nurture? And how do you nurture them without turning them off?

It's simple: You want to nurture every prospect who indicates potential interest in your services but doesn't have a current need.

That includes prospects who engage you but end up going with another writer, putting the project on hold or going in a different direction (e.g., hiring a full-time staff writer, hiring a content agency, etc.).

You should also nurture prospects who didn't go as far as to engage you but who contacted you about your services yet went completely silent before you were able to schedule a phone conversation.

A simpler way to look at it is to nurture *every* qualified prospect you come in contact with, *except the following:*

1. Prospects who, after some degree of follow-up, say flat out, "We have no interest or need for a writer."

2. Prospects who are not (or don't seem) qualified—either because you looked them up and can tell they wouldn't be a good prospect, or because after a conversation or email exchange you realized that they would not be a good fit.

What about everyone else? Does it really pay to stay in touch with NYR prospects? Check out these statistics and decide for yourself:

*   Forty-four percent of salespeople (as freelancers, we're selling our services, so we *are* salespeople!) give up after one follow-up. Yet 80% of sales require five follow-ups (sources: Scripted and Marketing Donut).

- Eighty percent of the prospects deemed "bad leads" by sales teams do go on to buy within 24 months (source: SiriusDecisions).

- On average, 15 to 20 percent of the "not yet ready to purchase" opportunities convert to sales [after lead nurturing] (source: Gleanster).

- Even inbound leads (inquiries) aren't as ready to act as most of us think! Sixty-three percent of people requesting information today about you and your services will not purchase for at least three months. And 20 percent will take more than 12 months to buy (source: Marketing Donut).

- Nurtured leads make 47 percent larger purchases than non-nurtured leads (source: The Annuitas Group).

- Lead-nurturing emails get four to 10 times the response rate compared with stand-alone email blasts (source: SilverPop/DemandGen Report).

So why the delay? Why do so many prospects take this long to make decisions? There are two key factors at play here: timing and trust.

Landing a new client requires both the right **timing** and a certain level of **trust**.

The timing for hiring you needs to be right. You can't create urgency inside the prospect's organization. But you *can* stay in touch until they're ready.

You also can't build trust overnight. It takes time, patience and a sincere desire to establish a meaningful connection with your prospects. To do that effectively, you need a smart, methodical and sincere lead-nurturing effort with your NYR prospects.

Think about a big personal purchase you've made—say, your first house. A family member knew you and your spouse were starting to think about buying a home, so she introduced you to her realtor, Peggy.

But maybe the timing wasn't right to hire Peggy. You needed time to save for a down payment. So you happily connected with Peggy, but you also told her that it was too early to go out looking for houses.

Peggy stayed in touch over the next few months, sending you an occasional article or relevant information on interest rates, sound advice for first-time home buyers and so on.

She wasn't pushy; she just kept in touch in a value-added way. Fourteen months later, when you had all your ducks in a row and were ready to get started, she was probably the first (and probably the only) realtor you contacted.

Makes sense, doesn't it?

But what if Peggy hadn't stayed in touch? Fourteen months is a long time. You may have forgotten about her. Or maybe you did remember her, but when you texted your relative asking her for Peggy's contact information, you never got a reply text. So you moved on.

Or Peggy could have gone about this the wrong way. She could have pressured you to start the buying process by emailing and calling you every month, asking "OK, are you ready now?"

So as you can see, it's easy to mess this up. You have to follow up. But you also have to do it right.

The Lead-Nurturing Process for NYR Prospects

There are four components to an effective lead-nurturing strategy:

1. Content library
2. Media
3. Frequency
4. Tracking and automation

Let's go through each one of these in more detail.

#1: Content Library

A huge factor in the success of your lead-nurturing efforts is adding value in every follow-up attempt. So you need good-quality content you can include in your follow-up messages.

What kind of content should you send? Here are some ideas:

Articles you've written. If you write a newsletter and have a few articles lying around from previous issues, move the best ones to your library.

Relevant, insightful and well-written self-authored articles make excellent nurturing material. They give you credibility, position you as an expert on the topic, and provide your prospects with ideas and insights that could help them do their jobs better.

Does your newsletter count? Yes, but you also need a personalized nurturing "layer" on top of your newsletter. You need that one-to-one communication, whereas a newsletter is one-to-many.

Reports or white papers. These can be powerful nurturing pieces. Here again, reports and white papers give you credibility while offering value to readers.

Don't have a report you can share? Not a problem! Try assembling one with previously published articles that touch on a common theme.

Useful and relevant tools and resources. Checklists, cheat sheets, templates, process maps, step-by-step plans, shortcuts, worksheets, scorecards or other tools you've created.

Don't have anything like that in your files? Why not create a few of these assets? I bet that in the course of your work you've developed internal checklists, processes, templates and other tools you use to write copy or content.

These might be things you do naturally, without thinking much about them. They're all in your head. But consider reverse engineering and documenting what you do. Yes, it takes time. But you'll end up with some very powerful tools you can use for multiple purposes, including as lead magnets and assets for your nurturing content library.

Success stories. Also known as "case studies" in marketing-speak, success stories are short articles that describe how you've helped a client solve a specific challenge and how the client specifically benefited from your service.

If you have one or two case studies already written, they can make fantastic nurturing material. If you don't have any but have a few client successes that would make for a great story, this may be a good time to approach those clients.

Third-party content. Your nurturing content library doesn't have to be completely self-authored. It's better to have a good mix of self-authored content and third-party information.

Assemble a good list of interesting and relevant third-party content in the way of articles, blog posts, reports, white papers, success stories, reference material, survey results and statistics.

You'll want to keep this library fresh and current, of course. But if you're reading up on your industry or craft on a regular basis, this won't be hard to do.

Books. If you work in a field in which each new client is worth thousands of dollars over the course of a year, you may want to consider adding books to your nurturing library. Pick books that are timely, relevant to the prospect, tied somehow to what you do and written by credible sources.

Books are memorable. After all, it's not every day that a prospect gets a free book in the mail, especially one that's relevant to their work.

Videos and podcasts. Whether it's a video you've put together with some practical and relevant tips, or a podcast you came across that would be relevant and valuable to your audience, rich media can be a great way to stay in touch while adding value.

Helpful tools. If you come across helpful and practical tools, apps, utilities, software or websites that would help your leads do their jobs more easily, add them to your library. Become the person who brings those valuable ideas to your prospects' attention. They won't forget you!

News stories or general announcements. Interesting news reports can work well. But so can general announcements about new things you're doing in your own business.

For instance, if you've recently partnered with another freelancer to deliver a more complete service, draft a one-page document that describes the service, lists all the deliverables, explains what's involved, describes your process or system, discusses the results clients can expect, and lists the advantages of using you instead of another provider.

Handwritten cards and other creative items. Get creative! Handwritten cards stand out in a world of electronic and mass-produced correspondence. The personal touch goes a long way toward staying top of mind with NYR prospects.

Where to find relevant information to add to your library:

- Industry publications, newsletters and blogs. Again, if you're keeping up with your industry, target market or craft, you'll automatically run into great content you can use for nurturing leads.

- Pocket (www.getpocket.com). This app enables you to "clip" and store articles and other content from the web. Once it learns your clipping patterns, it makes recommendations of relevant content you might like. Which makes it easier to find other great, relevant content.

- Crowdsourced content curation platforms such as www.inbound.org.

You'll want to keep a file with this content for easy access. I used to actually print and file my nurturing content. But these days I mainly use Evernote or Pocket.

Nine-word emails. So far we've only discussed using nine-word emails with dead leads and dormant clients. But once you have a nurturing list in place, it makes sense to throw the occasional nine-word email into the mix! Virtually any of the five flavors could work here, as long as you tailor it to the prospect, based on what you know about them.

Social media: Finally, connect with NYR and Ready prospects on social media (LinkedIn, Twitter and Facebook). And don't be all business all the time. Humanize yourself by posting updates about your life and what you're up to.

#2: Media

Using multiple media not only diversifies your efforts but also adds variety to your messages, which can help cut through the noise of junk mail and flooded email and voicemail inboxes.

There are three basic media you'll want to use in a rotating fashion:

Postal mail. Keep it simple. Stuff your printed nurturing piece into either a standard #10 envelope or yellow oversize envelope (a 9 x 12 envelope works). Include either a sticky note or a cardstock note with a personalized handwritten message, such as this:

> *Hi John,*
>
> *Came across this article recently.*
>
> *Thought you'd find it interesting.*
>
> *Ed*

Throw in your business card, hand-address the envelope and you're good to go! Few people ever get mail like this anymore, so your piece will stand out.

Email. It's efficient, recipients get emails right away and there's usually no gatekeeper, so the chances of getting through to prospects can be higher than with postal mail. The downside is that it could get lost in the shuffle and never read.

Phone. Throw a few phone calls into your nurturing mix. The telephone is a very personal and interactive medium. It humanizes you.

You can use the phone as a single nurturing touch point. Or you can use it as part of a "one-two punch" strategy to let the prospect know that you just emailed them something and wanted to give them a heads up.

Example of a good nurturing voicemail message:

Hi Jill.

Ed Gandia here. I'm the business-to-business copywriter you contacted back in December. I'm calling because I've recently worked with two clients to turn some of their white papers into one-sheet summaries for their sales teams.

This concept has really caught on with these two clients, and I thought it might be something you'd be interested in exploring.

If you'd like to connect, you can reach me at 770-555-1876 or ed@abcxyz.com.

Take care.

This one is simple, relaxed, sincere and to the point. And notice that even though it's obviously promotional in nature, there's value in there. It's not your typical "Hey, do you have anything for me?" message.

#3: Frequency

Remember: 44 percent of salespeople give up after one follow-up. Yet 80 percent of sales require five follow-ups (sources: Scripted and Marketing Donut).

That doesn't mean you call or email five times with an "Are you ready for me?" message. Five or more attempts means you stay in touch in a relevant and personalized way over a period of time.

The frequency and nature of your follow-up depend on:

- Stage of the sales cycle

- Who contacted whom

- Prospect's responsiveness and cues

- How long they've been on your nurturing list (the longer they've been on without any kind of response or acknowledgment, the lower the frequency)

Use these three factors to guide your decisions. But in general, sending something every one to three months is about right. Of course, you'll want to adjust that frequency up or down based on the three factors above. But when in doubt, use two months as your baseline frequency.

Something else that might help is to create and use a general sequence or protocol as a guide for what you'll send at each touch point. For example:

Date	Action/Deliverable
Month 1	Mail article of interest
Month 3	Touch base with a phone call/voicemail
Month 5	Email URL of results from an industry survey
Month 7	Mail client success story with a personal note
Month 9	Touch base with a phone call/voicemail
Month 11	Mail report or white paper with a sticky note attached
Month 13	Email URL of helpful checklist or self-assessment quiz
Month 15	Call to invite them to download a podcast
Month 17	Mail article of interest with a personal note
Month 19	Email URL of a relevant online video

These don't have to be set in stone. You could keep the descriptions more general and use the sequence as more of a guide than a strict protocol.

#4: Tracking and Automation

A simple spreadsheet will do when starting out with your nurturing program. Add a prospect per row and use a column to track what you sent that prospect (and when).

Once this activity becomes a habit, consider implementing a contact management system. Here are some popular options:

- www.highrisehq.com

- www.contactually.com

- www.zoho.com/crm

- www.hubspot.com/products/crm (this one is still free as of this writing!)

Resist the temptation to automate this process with emails or services such as "SendOutCards." Remember: The personal touch is key to effective follow-up!

Also, don't treat lead nurturing as a desperate attempt to convert a prospect to a client. Let go of any expectations and instead focus on sending relevant and personalized messages. Detaching yourself from a specific outcome is key.

Finally, understand that 80 percent compliance (good enough) is better than not starting your nurturing initiative because you want to get everything "just right" (perfection). So don't wait to act until you have it down perfectly.

Think "ready, fire, aim."

Chapter 4:

Your Action Plan

If you're anything like I am, you're probably wondering where you should start this process.

Or how you'll get this stuff done.

Or how you can possibly maintain some consistency when you're bound to get pulled in many different directions.

So let's address those concerns.

Take Care of the Big Rocks First

The late Stephen R. Covey described a scenario in his classic book *The 7 Habits of Highly Effective People* that has stayed with me ever since I first read it.

He described an exercise he'd do in his seminars that involved a bucket of big rocks, a bucket of gravel and a bucket of sand. A volunteer from the audience was tasked with emptying all three buckets into a large fishbowl.

Most volunteers started with the sand, pouring it into the fishbowl. They followed that with the gravel and the big rocks.

But by the time they got to the big rocks, there was no room in the fishbowl for half of them. The pebbles and the sand were taking up way too much room in the bowl!

Covey then explained that by reversing the order, you'd get very different results. So he brought out three new buckets and a new fishbowl. This time he asked the volunteer to start by placing the big rocks inside the fishbowl, then pour the gravel, then the sand.

Miraculously, the content of all three buckets fit this time. Why? Because once the big rocks were in, the sand and gravel could fit tightly in the crevices between the big rocks.

The lesson in this beautiful metaphor is that if we take care of all the little things first (the sand and gravel), there won't be enough room in our schedule for the important things—the big rocks. But when we schedule the important items into our week *first*, the little things somehow get done anyway.

So my first recommendation is simple: You have to schedule your prospecting into your week, much like you would, say, a doctor's appointment.

You wouldn't blow off a doctor's appointment just because you're running behind that day or because you don't feel like going, would you?

You'd find a way to make it happen!

So why would you blow off an appointment you made with yourself—and appointment that will help keep your business healthy?

Or why not treat your email prospecting as you would a client project? If you promised your client a first draft by next Friday—and you know that you have about four hours to go to complete that draft—you'd be wise to schedule those four hours into your calendar.

Prospecting requires the same kind of planning and discipline. You need to schedule it into your week ... and treat it like the "big rock" it is.

Create a Game Plan

Next, create a high-level game plan for yourself. As mentioned in the introduction, I strongly suggest that you follow this sequence:

1. Activate dead leads and dormant clients
2. Generate new leads
3. Nurture not-yet-ready leads

#1: Activate dead leads and dormant clients.

There's a very good reason to start with this group. You want to clear the decks of any potential opportunities. And everything else being equal, this group has the best probability of generating something for you quickly.

These people have already had contact with you. Some may even know and trust you already. So you don't have to start from scratch.

Contact each of your dead leads and dormant clients with a **nine-word email.**

Go through the different flavors from Chapter 1 and find the one you think would work best for each person. Don't overthink it. Go with your gut and get these emails out the door.

I suggest doing this in one sitting. That way you get the momentum and practice you need to make your nine-word emails more effective.

If you have a lot of dead leads and dormant clients to contact, schedule a bigger block of time. But don't put it off because you can't find a big block of time anytime soon. If that's an obstacle to getting started *this week*, break up this first effort into two or three sessions.

One more thing. If you don't get a response, there's no need to follow up—at least not right away. The objective of a nine-word email is to start a conversation. But if you get no response, trying again a few days later could backfire. Wait a few weeks and try again. Maybe with a different flavor or a different question.

#2: Generate new leads.

Once you've reached out to all your dead leads and dormant clients with a nine-word email, start reaching out to cold prospects in your target market with warm emails.

Again, don't worry about crafting the perfect email script. And don't spend hours researching each prospect. Instead, use the two categories of meaningful connections as your guide, keeping in mind that the idea is to show relevance and personalization.

Remember: It doesn't take much to show a prospect that you've done your homework. When 99 percent of every marketing email they get is a broadcast (or a broadcast pretending to be a one-to-one email), it's relatively easy to stand out with a short, personalized and relevant email.

#3: Nurture NYR leads.

As you start getting responses from dormant clients, dead leads and cold prospects, add qualified NYR leads to your nurturing list.

Note that once you've cleared the decks in step #1 with dead leads and dormant clients, the only recurring steps are #2 and #3.

Also note that nine-word emails could (and should!) be part of your nurturing effort. So don't forget about incorporating those into your nurturing sequences.

Turn Prospecting Into a Habit

Motivation and willpower are depletable resources. They get us started, *but they don't keep us going.* So if you're counting on them to help you prospect more consistently, you're going to be disappointed.

As the late motivational speaker Jim Rohn said: "Motivation is what gets you started. Habit is what keeps you going."

The only way you can ensure that your work pipeline will always be full is by developing a strong prospecting habit.

When we do something habitually, we think less. Our neurological activity actually decreases. That's why the behavior feels automatic.

Establish Designated Days

One powerful way to turn prospecting into a habit is to have designated days for certain activities. Once you've gone through all three steps and are down to prospecting and nurturing, consider assigning a theme to each day of the week. My friend Ilise Benun from www.marketing-mentor.com is a big proponent of this. I've found it to be extremely effective.

For instance, if you prefer to sprinkle your marketing efforts throughout the week, you might consider this schedule:

- Mondays: prospect research (1 hr.)
- Tuesdays: send warm emails (1 hr.)
- Wednesdays: send warm emails (1 hr.)
- Thursdays: nurture NYR leads (1 hr.)
- Fridays: work on my newsletter, blog or other content marketing (3 hrs.)

But if you prefer to focus your marketing efforts on certain days only, leaving you with more focused stretches for client work, this approach might work better:

- Mondays: prospect research + send warm emails (4 hrs.)
- Tuesdays: client work only
- Wednesdays: client work only
- Thursdays: client work only
- Fridays: nurture NYR leads + work on my content marketing (3 hrs.)

Besides giving you structure, this approach reduces the number of decisions you have to make on a daily basis. You can start each day knowing exactly what type of work you need to focus on.

One last tip: After experimenting with different approaches, I've found that it's best to focus on "effort" goals (e.g., how much time you'll dedicate to a certain activity each day) rather than on "outcome" goals (e.g., how many warm emails you'll send out that day)—especially when you're trying to build the habit.

What If You Get Off Track?

It's not uncommon to start this process with a high degree of motivation, only to fall behind the following week and end up discouraged.

What do you do then?

First, develop strategies for dealing with these mishaps. Develop an "if-then" strategy to get back on track before you slip up. Missing a habit one day has no impact on the long-term success of your habit—if you get back on track quickly.

Also, try to avoid the "all or nothing" mentality. This is a big issue with perfectionist personalities. Doing something small is better than doing nothing at all. The motivational boost you'll get from knowing that you at least took some action that day is priceless.

If you continue to have trouble getting your prospecting done, document your activities (including start and stop times) for two or three days so you can analyze how you're spending your time. Ask yourself: *What's happening here? What's truly keeping me from getting this done?*

Maybe you've overdone it—you've overscheduled yourself. If that's the case, don't beat yourself up. Instead, strip down your plan to the bare minimum. And don't feel guilty about it. But commit to getting back on track with this initiative. And once you're consistent with the stripped-down version, start adding to it incrementally.

A few more ideas:

- Build in some recovery time to make your habit more sustainable
- Take more breaks
- Adjust your plan as you go (better to adjust down than to do nothing)

Remember: Developing the habit is much more important than getting immediate results. It's the habit that's going to enable you to eventually meet those goals over the long haul.

Finally, if the reason for getting off track is that you're suddenly crazy-busy with client work, have a plan for that, too. Don't fall into the trap of thinking that you can avoid prospecting. Eventually the work will dry up, and you'll need a pipeline of projects to keep you going.

When you're overloaded with client work, you can shift gears without having to ignore your prospecting altogether. For instance, you could focus all your prospecting time on nurturing NYR clients rather than knocking on doors for work with cold prospects or dormant clients.

If an NYR prospect responds to your nurturing email with a project request, it won't feel strange to turn him or her down (or to ask the prospect if they can wait) because your email wasn't about asking for work. It was simply about staying in touch.

Start TODAY!

By far the most important thing you can do to start getting results with these ideas is start TODAY!

You don't have to start emailing today, but I implore you to do something right now, even if it's a small and simple action.

For example, you could look at the upcoming week and schedule two hours to contact your dead leads and dormant clients in one sitting.

Or you could spend 30 minutes today going through your contact list or contact management system to identify all dead leads and dormant clients.

Or maybe you use the examples in Chapter 1 to draft a handful of nine-word emails. You don't have to send them out today, but you'll at least have some ready to go.

The point: Do something now while you're motivated and thinking about this stuff. Don't risk forgetting about it.

Want Some Help?

Need some help deploying this email prospecting playbook in your business?

Better yet, want to work with me to double your freelance income over the next 12 to 18 months?

I've got a complete income-acceleration blueprint I'll walk you through. I'll help you deploy this blueprint in your own business. And I'll help keep you accountable throughout the process.

I've been doing this with established writers for nearly three years now. And the results have been pretty amazing. Very tangible.

If you'd like to explore how I may be able to do the same for you, send an email to **ed@b2blauncher.com** with the words "2X Coaching" in the subject line and I'll send you the details.

ABOUT THE AUTHOR

Ed Gandia is a business-building coach and strategist who helps freelancers earn more in less time doing work they love for better-paying clients.

He's the founder of High-Income Business Writing and Get Better Clients Academy, where he advises thousands of freelance professionals at all levels on how to deploy simple systems and frameworks for optimizing their business results.

Ed spent 12 years in corporate sales, where he developed repeatable strategies and processes for landing profitable deals faster and with less effort. He then applied many of these same approaches to his freelance copywriting business, enabling him to build a six-figure solo practice in 27 months.

Ed is the co-author of the bestselling book *The Wealthy Freelancer* and host of the top-ranked podcast High-Income Business Writing. His insights and rants have been featured in *Inc.* magazine, CNN Radio, CBS Radio News, *The Christian Science Monitor, The Atlanta Journal Constitution, DM News,* AirTran Airways' *Go* magazine and *The Writer,* among others.

He and his family live in suburban Atlanta, Georgia.

Made in the USA
San Bernardino, CA
07 March 2017